# BLESSING

## THE CULTURE OF GOD

## CHRISTIAN

### RAYMOND NGWU

**Blessing: The Culture of God**

For more information, visit www.bishopchris.com

Cover Design: Golgoth'art Communication

ISBN-13: 978-0692403587 (Bishop Chris)
ISBN-10: 0692403582

## ACKNOWLEDGEMENTS

Heartfelt appreciation to...

Craig Hill for all his books, which have been a great and continuous source of edification.

My staff, who work tirelessly to make us appear our best even when that is not obvious.

My editor, Minister Yvan Amatagana, for making this book an enjoyable and gratifying read.

Pastors Victor Naibi and Victor Itambon of RHEMA Publication, for making the printing of this book possible.

My technical assistant, Kingsley Tabifor, for a great cover design and for transcribing the manuscript.

**And thank you Precious Holy Spirit for your leadership and inspiration.**

## ABBREVIATIONS

HCSB: Holman Christian Standard Bible
KJV: The Bible, King James Version
NKJV: New King James Version
RSV: Revised Standard Version

# TABLE OF CONTENTS

ACKNOWLEDGEMENTS................................................................iii
ABBREVIATIONS......................................................................iv
TABLE OF CONTENTS................................................................v

INTRODUCTION | EMBRACING GOD'S CULTURE.....................1

CHAPTER ONE | UNDERSTANDING THE BLESSING................5

CHAPTER TWO | DISTINGUISHED BY THE BLESSING..........20

CHAPTER THREE | ACTIVATING THE BLESSING ..................36

CHAPTER FOUR | ESTABLISHING THE CULTURE OF
BLESSING ...............................................................................57

CHAPTER FIVE | HINDRANCES TO THE BLESSING..............86

FINAL WORDS.........................................................................93

About the author.....................................................................97

# INTRODUCTION

## EMBRACING GOD'S CULTURE

Culture refers to the way a person, a people, a group or a nation thinks, behaves and works. Culture is ubiquitous, inevitable, subtly influencing the fate of all humans. It shapes a person's destiny by dictating their thought and behavioral patterns: "For as a man thinks in his heart, so is he" (Proverbs 23:7).

In like manner, God's dealings with His creatures are founded on a unique culture that He has framed for Himself, and which flows from His nature. The nature of God is a compound of beauty, splendor, blessedness and goodness, and blessing is probably the most spontaneous outward expression of that nature. Blessing is his culture, how he expresses who he is.

Therefore, anybody who is going to represent God must know and embrace this truth. You must know that you are called to propagate a culture on the earth called blessing. You must strive towards that in spite of what everybody around you might say.

Understanding the power and importance of blessing and upholding it as a culture can transform an entire life, church or nation. If your children are blessed, there will be less cursing and less evil. There will be less of all the negative things which plague the world. The more you are blessed, the lesser you have time for negative things and the more you can help other people.

Unfortunately, the Church has embraced a culture that is contrary to God's. Most believers have been taught that God's blessing is an elusive reality that one can access only on special conditions. For this reason, the Church has emphasized and amplified the issues of sin and death, instead of amplifying good things. Most preachers think they are missing out if they keep preaching blessing, glory and growth without teaching failure, sickness and sin as well. Some even go as far as claiming that balance requires preaching the good and the bad because energy comes by a blend of both positive and negative charges. How absurd!

The Bible says in Galatians 5:16 that we should walk in the Spirit so we shall not fulfill the desires of the flesh. It is the emphasis on the Spirit that overcomes the flesh, not the other way round. It is high time the Church started emphasizing the blessedness of the believer and communicating that blessing to her world. The Church exists to be the ultimate manifestation of God's blessing on the earth and the ultimate messenger of His culture.

Once established, culture functions on auto-play; once anchored in the mind, it bears fruit automatically. The purpose of this book is to urge the Church at all levels—individual, congregational, national and global—to move away from unproductive man-made cultures into God's very own culture, and then influence the world. This is a journey that we must embark on deliberately.

Now, I have seen a vision. I have seen the day when this divine culture becomes a reality in our families and communities. This is no suggestion but a proclamation of God's mind. You are either going to preach God or preach something else and fail your generation and the Kingdom you are supposed to represent. The culture of God is blessing, beyond any argument, and I challenge anyone to prove otherwise. If you embrace and practice this culture, you will enjoy it.

Let the journey begin.

# CHAPTER ONE

## UNDERSTANDING THE BLESSING

The word "blessing", as rendered from the Hebrew *barakah*, means "good things spoken" or simply "benediction." In the New Testament, the verb "to bless" is translated from the Greek word *eulogeo*, which means "to speak well of" and "to cause to prosper". Another Greek word, used in the Beatitudes, describes the blessedness of one approved by God: *makarios*, which means "well off", "happy", "fortunate", or "supremely blessed".

Genesis 1:28 says:

*Then God **blessed** them, and God **said** to them,"Be fruitful and multiply; fill the earth and subdue it; have dominion over the fish of the sea, over the birds of the air, and over every living thing that moves on the earth.*

Blessing is goodness, ability and favor released through saying—the spoken word. Matthew 12: 34b says, "For out of the abundance of the heart the mouth speaks." Hence, blessing is that which comes from the bowels of God, which is Goodness itself, which God confers upon a being by speaking. Every benevolent characteristic of God which is released upon a person is called blessing.

Blessing is that attribute of God that makes Him God and causes things to happen, especially for good. The word "God" means "Divine Goodness" and when he imputes that goodness on someone it is called a blessing.

*Every good gift and every perfect gift is from above, and comes down from the Father of lights, with whom there is no variation or shadow of turning. (James 1:17)*

Blessing is that which God gives of Himself or,

would I say, what He speaks of Himself over a being. It is his declaration of what the identity of a life should be.

## The power and purpose of blessing

Blessing brings supernatural empowerment to the life of the receiver. In John 6:63, the Lord Jesus says, "The words that I speak to you are spirit and they are life." Blessing is essentially the energy to produce good. It is the potency to produce results.

*The blessing of the LORD,* **it maketh rich,** *and he addeth no sorrow with it.* Proverbs 10:22 KJV

*And you shall remember the Lord your God, for it is He who gives you* **power to get** *wealth, that He may establish His covenant which He swore to your fathers, as it is this day.* Deuteronomy 8:18.

This "power to get" is the Blessing. As a matter of fact, blessing is what secures life on earth. It is to life what fuel is to a car engine: the oil that runs it and the energy that quickens it.

Blessing is not cars, houses, spouses, children,

diamond rings, etc. While in our Christian parlance these material and earthly goodies are widely referred to as "blessings", they actually are not blessings. The blessing is not the things themselves, but rather an endowment, a force that enables one to get all these things and much more.

Another look at Proverbs 10:22 in the *Holman Christian Standard Bible* reveals yet another powerful fact: "The LORD's blessing enriches, **and struggle adds nothing to it**". This rendition makes it clear that the blessing of the Lord is a force that enables you to achieve results that you could never have attained by your natural strength and efforts. Blessing empowers you for a life that is bigger than what your strength, background and circumstances would normally afford.

That said, you MUST be blessed. It is mandatory if you are going to enjoy life and live meaningfully. The normal Christian life is a blessed life.

In Genesis, God blessed man by endowing him with the power to multiply, subdue, and replenish. It is this original blessing God declared over MAN –

not just believers – that is responsible for all the artistic, scientific and technological advances the world has achieved so far. God, by just one sentence, empowered humans to reign supreme over all other creatures of the earth.

If the Church understands this, and decides to claim and practice blessing on purpose, it is only a matter of time before some of the greatest inventions and innovations of our time start popping up from within the Body of Christ. Here is what the Bible says in Micah 4:1:

*In the last days the mountain of the LORD's house will be established at the top of the mountains and will be raised above the hills. Peoples will stream to it.* HCSB

How is this going to happen? It is the blessing that will take us there! It is high time believers be credited with developing new and more efficient economic models, educational systems, ground-breaking technology, and life-saving vaccines. And this will all be made possible through the blessing of God.

At the level of our families and communities, a

parent's blessing will make a tremendous difference in the lives of their children. By blessing your spouse and kids, you can secure their future, safeguard their destiny, ensure their salvation, and fill their pockets. Releasing multiple blessings over one another as a couple will promote long-lasting peace in the home, as you can't hate someone you keep on blessing all the time. There is no limit to what the blessing can do!

Blessing powers life. It makes us productive and successful in all things in life. Neglect of the blessing is neglect of the power of God that is capable of changing situations for us. Strange enough, when people set their minds to pursue this blessed, empowered life, we label them as carnal. This is because we ourselves have lived a carnal life in the disguise of the Spirit. We have lived a life void of the power of God. That is what carnality is: a life void of the power of God. Consequently, the Church has not really entered into her blessed identity. We have lived for ourselves based on our own interpretation of blessings as money, houses, marriage, children and so on. But what is the purpose of these things?

If you are living a healthy life, what are you living for? In Job 38, God asked Job, among other things, what he had achieved in his long life, especially given that he had been so blessed.

This means that blessings have a purpose. They are meant to engineer something. They are there to keep your creativity going. Your godlikeness prospers by the blessing of God. That is the reason for blessing: that the nature of God—that creative, innovative and inventive part in us—should flourish.

## The universality of blessing

God's perfect will is for *all* humans to enjoy the blessing. Blessing actually predated redemption, meaning that before there ever was a fall, and before the Savior was manifested on planet earth, God had blessed MAN—and He has not changed His mind ever since. The capacity to bless and be blessed is a privilege given to all humans, born again or not.

Both Jews and Christians have struggled with this truth because they believe God is their private property. While the latter do enjoy a unique position and inheritance with God, God can't be theirs alone and no one else's. Failing to realize that God's mind is not just full of Christians but full of MAN has robbed many believers of the opportunity to be channels of blessings to the world — because they assume that if you don't belong to their church and do certain things, you cannot be blessed.

How far can you be from the truth? Blessing was not your engineering, and your religion is not the pioneer of it. Just as God blessed Jesus before He started ministering, saying "This is My Son in whom I AM well pleased," so does ANY father have the authority to empower his children's lives by uttering positive declarations over them.

*What is **man** that You are mindful of him, And the son of man that You visit him?* Psalms 8:4.

*LORD, what is **man**, that thou takest knowledge of him! or the son of man, that thou makest account of him!* Psalms 144:3.

So we must understand this passion God has for mankind as a whole and acknowledge that if all men can be blessed, then those who are in God should exceedingly abound in blessings (Proverbs 28:20). In other words, blessing can multiply because you have a special relationship with God, but you cannot tell anybody that they cannot be blessed because they are not a Christian. No one can legislate the blessing of God because blessing is a human right.

*The heavens are the LORD's heavens, but the earth he has given to the sons of men.* Psalms 115:16 RSV

We Christians therefore should not develop an elitist, us-alone mindset, which might cause us to cut off from the world into our own Christian schools, hospitals and businesses where a Muslim for example cannot feel comfortable.

I am by no means saying that I am against those manifestations of our faith; I am rather emphasizing that our Christianity is better shown by our ability to love the unlovable, to like the unlikable. What is our Christian testimony? The apostle Paul tells us in Romans 5:7-8:

*For scarcely for a righteous man will one die; yet perhaps for a good man someone would even dare to die.*

*But God demonstrates His own love toward us, in that while we were still sinners, Christ died for us.*

And as the Father sent Jesus, so has He sent us. We are not supposed to show less. As Christians, we are not supposed to keep our faith and blessedness to ourselves; we are to share it freely with the world. God wants us to contaminate the world with His blessing. He wants us to demonstrate and release his blessing to our families, communities and nations: this is part of bringing heaven on earth.

## The origins of blessing

Blessing did not start with man but with God, not as an expression of what God had to do after He made man, but simply because that is who He is. Blessing is not something that you thought of or the outcome of some good thing that you did. It is a state of being that originated in God. That is why when God initiated life, He had to ensure its continuity by giving part of Himself, which is the blessing.

Moreover, we have to understand that man was

not the first creature to be blessed on the earth; fish and trees were. Is it not strange then, that man is now trying to pursue blessing as though it were something that was designed and thought of only when he came? In Genesis 1, we saw that as soon as the waters were asked to bring forth fish, God blessed them and told them to multiply. And this is the same thing He said to the animals. So the origin of blessing is from God. We must understand that if we keep things in their proper perspective we will struggle less with this truth. A blessing is something wonderful that should not be the exclusive preserve of a few who get it while others don't.

For me, the biblical origin of blessing is simple: God. It started and emanated from God and eventually flows back to God. Like the popular song goes:

*"Amen, Amen, blessings and glory, wisdom, thanksgiving and honor, power and might belong to our God, forever and ever, Amen!"*

We take back to Him that which came from Him.

## The unconditionality of blessing

We should realize that blessings are unconditional. As soon as living creatures began to appear in the waters, God blessed them with the power to multiply, as revealed in the book of Genesis:

*And God created great whales, and every living creature that moves, which the waters brought forth abundantly, after their kind, and every winged fowl after his kind: and God saw that it was good.*

*And God blessed them, saying, be fruitful, and multiply, and fill the waters in the seas, and let fowl multiply in the earth.* Genesis 1:21-22

Can you imagine God, who blessed the fish, refusing to bless man who is far more important than the fish of the sea? When man was created in verse 26 of the same chapter, he did not do anything to deserve the blessing. The blessing was a prerequisite for his existence. Hence, God blessed him by default, not by virtue of his righteousness or his works. God did not bless a Christian; He blessed a Man.

However, even though blessings are unconditional, there are qualities that expose you to a higher degree of blessedness, including knowledge, fellowship with God, and faithfulness. We shall see this in more detail in a later chapter.

## KEY POINTS

- Blessing is God's idea.

- Blessing is good things spoken over a person's life. When of God, it is God's goodness coming over a person to empower them.

- Blessing is the engine that powers life. The normal Christian life is a blessed life.

- Blessing is not things or achievements; it is the power to get and achieve.

- Blessing is God's default way of dealing with His creatures.

- Blessing empowers you for a life that is bigger than what your own strength, background and circumstances would normally afford.

- Blessing is unconditional because God blessed the first man before he ever did anything.

- Blessing is universal: Anyone can bless and be blessed, including non-believers.

- Blessing can also be provoked by one's deeds and faithfulness.

- We must contaminate the world with God's blessings.

# CHAPTER TWO

## DISTINGUISHED BY THE BLESSING

Christianity is supposed to be the manifestation of the superior preference God has placed over His people. One of the reasons the unsaved are not yet flooding into our move is because the difference between us and them is not yet evident. Of course, they have seen us martyred for our faith but the Christian life is not summarized in us suffering for God. If that is the case, then our faith is not complete. The testimony of the Lord in 2 Timothy

2:12 is that if you suffer with Him, you will also reign with Him. He did not say when you die; He said you will reign with Him in this life. Dominion means that you are in charge, you are the influence, and you are the voice.

Christians must take charge of all domains from education to religion, to arts and culture. The world must get to a place where when someone is saying the last word, it is a Christian who is saying it. So far, a large percentage of the inventions on this earth in all aspects of life, came from Jews. Many of the most successful entrepreneurs the world has known were of Jewish descent. Scores of books have been written in an attempt to decipher and explain the mystery behind their staggering success. Just look at the following list of some of the most influential Jews in history, and you will better understand what I am talking about:

- Albert Einstein, physicist;
- Sigmund Freud, psychiatrist;
- Karl Marx and Spinoza, philosophers;
- Steven Spielberg, filmmaker;
- Bob Dylan, musician;

- Jerry Siegel and Joe Shusterb, comics book artist/writer, creators of Superman;
- Emile Durkheim, sociologist;
- Henry Kissinger, politician;
- Marcel Proust, novelist;
- Arthur Miller, playwright;
- Sergey Brin, Co-founder of Google;
- And the list goes on endlessly.

Now consider some of the most famous quotes about the Jewish people below:

*If statistics are right, the Jews constitute but one percent of the human race. It suggests a nebulous dim puff of stardust lost in the blaze of the Milky Way. Properly, the Jew ought hardly to be heard of, but he is heard of, has always been heard of. He is as prominent on the planet as any other people, and his commercial importance is extravagantly out of proportion to the smallness of his bulk. His contributions to the world's list of great names in literature, science, art, music, finance, medicine, and abstruse learning are also away out of proportion to the weakness of his numbers. He has made a marvelous fight in this world, in all the ages; and has done it with his hands tied behind him.* **Mark Twain**

*Some people like the Jews, and some do not. But no thoughtful man can deny the fact that they are, beyond any question, the most formidable and most remarkable race which has appeared in the world.* **Winston S. Churchill**

*Considering their small numbers, Jews have fared disproportionately well in lists of the world's most powerful and richest people, as well as in Nobel Prizes.*

*The world Jewish population is estimated at being 0.2 percent of the total populace – some 13.5 million, with just over 5.7 million in Israel, 5.6 million in the US, half a million in Russia and France, 280,000 in the UK and 200,000 in Germany.*

*Yet in Vanity Fair's latest list of the 100 most powerful people in the world, 51 are Jews. Ten of the 50 people on this year's Forbes' annual billionaires list are Jewish. Of the 802 Nobel prizes handed out to date, 162 have gone to Jews.*

*In Michael H. Hart's book, The 100: A Ranking of the Most Influential Persons in History, seven are Jews.*

*Jews have also featured prominently on Time's annual list of the world's 100 most influential people, and in 1999, the magazine named Albert Einstein person of the century.* **The Jerusalem Post, May 21, 2010 Issue.**

This is simply mind-blowing. And yet, the Bible reveals to us that Christians are the only set of people on the earth that the Jews will ever envy or be jealous of:

*I say then, Have they stumbled that they should fall? God forbid: but rather through their fall salvation is come unto the Gentiles, for to provoke them to jealousy.* **Romans 11:11 KJV**

The Jews believe in their uniqueness, in their "chosenness" and in their blessedness, which are rooted in their identity as descendants of Abraham. But there is a breed of people that are more chosen and blessed than the Jews. The Bible says in 1 Peter 2:9-10 that we, believers, are a chosen generation, a peculiar people, and a royal priesthood. Look at how beautifully the Message Bible puts it:

*But you are the ones chosen by God, chosen for the high calling of priestly work, chosen to be a holy people, God's instruments to do his work and speak out for him, to tell others of **the night-and-day difference he made for you**—from nothing to something, from rejected to accepted.*

Christians must get to a place where people will look around and realize they cannot do without these Christ followers because they are the ones improving life here on earth. Our scientists must get to work because the hidden heritage of the earth is ours. Now, in Christ, this blessing spoken over the tribe of Zebulun, descendants of Abraham, should become our reality:

*They shall call the people unto the mountain; there they shall offer sacrifices of righteousness: for they shall suck of **the abundance of the seas**, and of **treasures hid in the sand**.* **Deuteronomy 33:19 KJV**

There is an abundance reserved for Believers to enjoy, and there are hidden treasures waiting to be unearthed by us, equations to be deciphered, and inventions to be made. The Bible also says in Colossians 2:3 that, in Christ "are hid all the treasures of wisdom and knowledge". There are treasures—both physical and intellectual—that are still left for us to discover, but we do not appropriate and experience this reality because we do not understand our blessedness. Our identity is ignored, so we cannot make discoveries.

### Blessed but not aware

As amply illustrated earlier, the Jews have progressed more than any other race on the earth so far. The Israelites have a proclivity to believe that they are more blessed as a people than all other races on earth, and as of now, nothing proves otherwise. But that can be far from the truth. Christians are more blessed, technically, because they have received the Messiah which the Jews rejected.

But here is the paradox: how come the ones who already have him are living a less productive life than the ones who are still expecting him to come? The reason is simple:

*Therefore my people are gone into captivity, because they have no knowledge: and their honourable men are famished, and their multitude dried up in thirst.* Isaiah 5:13

This point is further amplified in Psalm 49:20:

*A man that is in honour and knows it not is like a beast in the field that perishes.*

So it does not matter who you are or what your heritage is, if you do not know that you have it, you will not enjoy it.

The story is told of a man who paid a first-class

ticket to travel in a prestigious ship but traveled starving and in penury because he never knew that even the food was included with the ticket. Ignorance is no excuse before the law.

The rest of God's people, especially the Christians, are in penury because they have little knowledge about their inheritance and culture. The Christian culture is still based on survival! That is not supposed to be the case. The Christian culture should be the heritage of God. God is our heritage, and Jehovah is our Father. The One everybody else calls God is *our* Father.

Still, we have no culture that mimics His. We just pray prayers that are not even consistent with God's mind. Some of our best prayers are still focused on deliverance from the things He has freed us from some 2,000 years ago. Can you imagine that the people who are the heirs of this earth are living in penury and irrelevance? I am talking about the ones mentioned in Romans 5:17, which says they shall reign with Christ on this earth. This scripture is not real in their life because they are not even expecting it to happen. They are expecting to reign with Him when they die. God cannot do anything with someone who doesn't know. Jesus said it in a rash way: "you don't take your pearls and cast it before dogs."

We have dogs as pets, and that is good, but when you cast a pearl before a dog, it cannot understand its value. When it bites the pearl and finds it is hard, it will think it's a trap and will angrily turn around and attack you. A lot of Christians are like that. When you teach them about their blessedness in Christ, they attack you, accusing you of making Christianity cheap and encouraging them to live in sin. They will question your message, complaining that if this is the way of life God wants them to embrace, why then have they been living strict, ordered, ascetic lives and all the like. An ordered life has nothing to do with who you are. Your blessing is your identity. The things you do with your life rather have to do with your destiny. Knowing the difference between the two is essential.

Meanwhile, the average Jew is taught that Abraham is his Father and that he is the heir of the earth—not just Palestine. That is why those who are fighting for Palestine are wasting time and energy. The Jew fighting for Palestine is just fighting for his homeland. His heritage is the earth. The Jews who are ruling the earth right now are not in Palestine, but all over the world!

Now Christians are the sons of Abraham not only by promise but by the better covenant, the fulfillment of the law and the prophets. However, they are taught that they have no right to the benefits of this covenant, and therefore should not expect to experience them. Somehow, they are given the impression that if they set their heart on the blessing, it makes them more carnal than spiritual.

That's the reason you see honest Christians who are leading a strict life and wallowing in absolute penury, with broken marriages, kids forsaking the Christian faith and compromising in outrageous ways. But we must reject this lie and claim our inheritance in Abraham today! The blessing given to Abraham is ours in Christ, and it must become our belief and experience.

## The Judaic Error

The error Christians are making nowadays in trying to walk in blessings is to step into Judaism. They are trying to bring Judaism into Christianity. There are more "Judaizers" in Christendom today and Paul says in Galatians that if you do that you are accursed, severed from the grace that is in Christ. As much as we love the Jews (because our roots are in the Jews—for Jesus was a Jew), we are not "Judaizers" and should not in any way practice their religion.

What would make a normal Jew jealous of Jesus except for heaven and hell? It is not the miracles, because even though our Lord performed unprecedented miracles, the Hebrew people had at least seen many great ones throughout their history with God. The question now is, since Christ left, how much of his ways have we been practicing? To make matters worse, Jesus went to the Father so that we can do greater works, taking His legacy from glory to glory. To what extent have we done this? How far have we taken His agenda?

We have to establish a culture that can go from generation to generation, a culture that will cause people to say there must be something about these Christians. Nothing ever goes wrong in their lives. Nothing ever is misplaced in their lives. This is the culture of blessing. He became a curse so that the blessing of Abraham could be made available to us as part of a new, better covenant.

Now, instead of focusing on that and emulating the principles applied by those who, as of now, have enjoyed the blessing of Abraham the most on the earth, many Christians rather tend to copy the outward, physical aspects of the Hebrew religion. For instance, there is nothing wrong with using the *shofar*, but do we have to make it a doctrine? How many of our people today are using it in prayer? Many Christians today want to wear the *talib* and the prayer shawl, while others are celebrating all the Jewish feasts including the *Yom Kippur*. I have nothing against anyone doing Passover, Pentecost, Feast of the Tabernacle, and so on, but we need to understand that all these feasts and objects point to spiritual realities that we can access without necessarily using the same forms and rites. I have nothing against all of that because the Jews are my root, but their religion is not mine and does not answer for my salvation. So really, we are desirous of what they have whereas we have something far better: the very Grace of Jesus-Christ that gives us access to God's entire economy.

## The value of Grace

Let us not compromise what we have, for that is what the world needs. We are recipients of God's superabundant Grace. And this Grace is not just unmerited favor, as the widely known simplistic definition would put it. Grace encapsulates all of God's goodness released to man through His Son Jesus-Christ. Grace is divine enablement; it is divine bias that marks an individual for distinction above others. God will have nothing more to give to the world after Grace. Grace is the last thing God has according to Scriptures. Grace is what will take us back to eternity. Grace is what will sustain eternity. After grace, there is nothing else. Nothing can be added to Grace for eternity. That is the revelation and depth of God. Sadly, we, the custodians of this mystery, are living beside it. Let us call Christians back to this order. We are called to reign in this life by Christ, and we are empowered to do so by the abundance of Grace we have received.

*For if by one man's offence death reigned by one; much more they which receive abundance of grace and of the gift of righteousness shall reign in life by one, Jesus Christ.* **Romans 5:17 KJV**

With that in mind, there are useful habits in Judaism that we can learn from and import into our Christian culture, especially their consistency in making sure that generationally and seasonally, their children are blessed. The Jews are very consistent with generational blessings. Christians, on the contrary, have been bothered only about generation curses. Bear this in mind: as Christians, we possess the greatest treasure and inheritance in the whole universe—Christ in us, the hope of glory!

## KEY POINTS

- Christianity is supposed to be the manifestation of the superior preference God has placed over His people.
- Christians are the only set of people on the earth that the Jews will ever envy or be jealous of.
- The Jews are very consistent with generational blessings. Christians, on the contrary, have been bothered only about generation curses.
- Christians must get to a place where people will turn around and realize they cannot do without these Christ followers because they are the ones improving life here on earth.
- The blessing given to Abraham is ours in Christ, and it must become our belief and our experience.
- Grace encapsulates all of God's goodness released to man through His Son Jesus-Christ. Grace is divine enablement; it is divine bias that marks an individual

for distinction above others.

- We are called to reign in this life by Christ, and we are empowered to do so by the abundance of Grace we have received.

- Jesus went to the Father so that we can do greater works, taking His legacy from glory to glory.

- Jewish feasts and religious items point to spiritual realities that we can access without necessarily using the same forms and rites.

# CHAPTER THREE

## ACTIVATING THE BLESSING

*Christ hath redeemed us from the curse of the law, being made a curse for us: for it is written, Cursed is every one that hangeth on a tree:*
*That the blessing of Abraham might come on the Gentiles through Jesus Christ; that we might receive the promise of the Spirit through faith.* Galatians 3:13-14 KJV

As children of God, we must understand that we ARE blessed—not future tense, but right now. In

Christ, the blessing of Abraham became ours.

For unjustifiable reasons, however, most of the Christian Church still frowns at the notion of blessing, preferring to emphasize a timid message which they believe will help believers make heaven. Meanwhile, if you are a true believer in Christ Jesus, you are already in heaven, and God has kept us here on earth so we can represent Him and share the blessedness of being in Him with our world: bringing His will, His standard, His ingenuity on earth, even in the midst of the growing challenges our communities are facing today.

God has blessed us in a unique way in Christ Jesus, and He wants us to experience His blessing and impact our world with it. We are called to model and preach the *Good* News, aren't we? News of blessing and not of curse, news of acceptance and not of rejection, news of freedom and not of bondage, news of all-round prosperity and not of poverty. It is high time the Church woke up to this calling and started releasing blessings rather than curses all over the place – unapologetically.

Now, as an individual believer, you need to understand your blessedness and learn how to walk in the reality of it in your life, so you can better communicate it to those around you.

Blessing must become your culture, your daily lifestyle, not a one-time manifestation conferred on you through the prayer of your man of God. Even though someone can release or unlock the blessing over your life, it is up to you to learn to walk in it daily. Blessing is unconditional, freely given to us through the grace of our Lord Jesus. But you need to believe it, activate it, and cultivate it. God has designed life to be powered by the blessing. In the following lines, I am going to show you how to go about it.

## FOUNDATIONS OF A BLESSED LIFE

In order to walk in the blessing, you need to understand two major foundational components, namely identity and choice.

### i. Identity

Blessing is tied to identity and is, therefore, unconditional. We are ultimately blessed by virtue of who we are in Him, not by virtue of what we have done for Him. Again, while our actions can also provoke blessings, we had no part whatsoever in God's original decision to lavish us with His Goodness. In fact, it is His blessing that enables us to do anything we will ever do for Him or our world.

Acknowledging that you are blessed simply by virtue of who you are in Him is essential, and yet many believers miss it. While every Jew believes he is blessed on the basis of his identity as a descendant of Abraham, Christians struggle with believing that they are blessed by virtue of their identity in Christ. But here is what the Scripture says:

*Know ye therefore that they which are of faith, the same*

*are the **children of Abraham.***

*And the scripture, foreseeing that God would justify the heathen through faith, preached before the gospel unto Abraham, saying, **In thee** shall all nations be blessed.*

*So then **they which be of faith** are blessed with faithful Abraham.* Gal 3:7-9 KJV

*Blessed be the God and Father of our Lord Jesus Christ, who hath blessed us with all spiritual blessings in heavenly places **in Christ.*** Ephesians 1:3 KJV

*And if ye be Christ's, then are ye **Abraham's seed**, and heirs according to the promise.* Gal 3:29 KJV

The phrases "children of Abraham", "in thee", "they which be of faith", "in Christ", and "Abraham's seed" all refer to identity. Because we are Abraham's children, we are blessed. Because we are in Christ, we are blessed with the inheritance reserved for his seed. Understanding this will make life easier, because when your identity is secure everything follows suit without effort.

## ii. Choice

*I call heaven and earth as witnesses against you today that I have set before you life and death, blessing and curse. Choose life so that you and your descendants may live.* Deuteronomy 30:19 HCSB

Everything in God's economy hinges on choice. Life and blessing will not be imposed on you. You will enjoy it only if you deliberately go for it and decide that it *must* be your experience.

Choosing also entails desiring. Do you really want to see God's blessing become a reality in your life? Or are you satisfied with struggling on your own without this divine empowerment? It is up to you to decide. You must become addicted to the blessing and desire it earnestly—and make no apologies about it. Be addicted to it until it becomes your habit, then your character, then your everyday reality.

## ACTIVATING THE BLESSING

Once you have a hold of identity and choice, you can activate the blessing by developing certain habits and attitudes.

### #1. Acknowledge your blessedness

*That the communication of thy faith may become effectual by the **acknowledging** of every good thing which is in you in Christ Jesus.* **Philemon 1: 6 KJV**

*I pray that your participation in the faith may become effective through **knowing** every good thing that is in us for the glory of Christ.* **Philemon 1: 6 HCSB**

*So, you too consider yourselves dead to sin but alive to God in Christ Jesus.* **Romans 6: 11 HCSB**

Until you know and acknowledge the good things that are yours in Christ Jesus, the communication or participation of your faith—meaning your Christian walk—will not be effective. Until you are cognizant of what God has freely given you in Christ, your blessedness will not become your reality on earth.

Now, after having mentioned how God has blessed us in Ephesians 1: 3, let's take a closer look at verses 5 to 14 to discover some of the spiritual favors God has graced us with in Christ, highlighted for easy identification.

*Having predestinated us unto the* **adoption** *of children by Jesus Christ to himself, according to the good pleasure of his will, To the praise of the glory of his grace, wherein he hath made us* **accepted** *in the beloved. In whom we have* **redemption** *through his blood, the* **forgiveness** *of sins, according to the riches of his grace; Wherein he hath abounded toward us in all* **wisdom and prudence***; Having made known unto us* **the mystery of his will***, according to his good pleasure which he hath purposed in himself: That in the dispensation of the fullness of times he might gather together in one all things in Christ, both which are in heaven, and which are on earth; even in him: In whom also we have obtained an* **inheritance***, being predestinated according to the purpose of him who worketh all things after the counsel of his own will: That we should* **be to the** *praise of his glory, who first trusted in Christ. In whom ye also trusted, after that ye heard the word of truth, the gospel of your salvation: in whom also after that ye believed, ye were **sealed with that Holy Spirit** of promise, Which is the earnest of our inheritance until the redemption of the purchased possession, unto the praise of his glory.* (KJV)

The highlighted portions are just some of the amazing spiritual blessings Jesus has secured for us in heavenly places. Remember, the spiritual controls the physical, meaning that each of these blessings will have enormous impact over the outcome of your earthly experience—if only you can grasp them. Can you picture how being **adopted**, **accepted**, **redeemed** and **forgiven by God himself** can possibly impact on your destiny here on earth? How about the blessings of **wisdom and prudence**, an **inheritance** and **being sealed with the Holy Spirit**? God's extravagant goodness towards us means that failure and meaninglessness are totally out of the question for anyone who dares believe. These spiritual blessings guarantee the fulfillment of the promise given to Abraham:

*And I will make of thee a great nation, and I will bless thee, and make thy name great; and thou shalt be a blessing.* **Gen 12: 2 KJV**

It is therefore critical that you get to know God's word intimately in order to be able to enforce the inheritance that is rightfully yours by declaring it in faith. "My people are destroyed for lack of knowledge," Hosea 4: 6 warns. You cannot claim an inheritance you have not even heard of. You cannot enjoy a privilege you are not aware of.

## #2. Declare your blessedness

The second step to activating the blessing in your life is declaration. The Bible says that life and death are in the power of the tongue. Someone also noted that a closed mouth equals a closed destiny. You must declare over yourself everything you know is rightfully yours in Christ Jesus.

*We having the same spirit of faith, according as it is written, I believed, and therefore have I spoken; we also believe, and therefore speak.* 2 Corinthians 4: 13 KJV.

Dear friend, if you believe anything, speak it! Do not keep your mouth shut. Now go ahead and declare these blessings over your life:

- I am blessed by nature.
- I am blessed and highly favored!
- The imaginations of my mind are blessed.
- Out of me shall flow rivers of living water.
- In health and personality, I shall be strong like the baobabs of Africa.
- The works of my hands are blessed.
- My children are top amongst their equals and shall be distinguished in their generation.
- I am the heir of the earth. I will eat of its fatness.
- The doors of destiny open before me.
- I am the apple of God's eye and anyone or anything that comes against me shall be crushed in Jesus' name.
- I am wired to create and to dominate the creations of God; therefore, my authority is

affirmed.

In Jesus' name!

Until such things become your daily declaration, you will only enjoy a tiny share of all life has in store for you.

## TRIGGERS OF THE BLESSING

Once the foundation is established through acceptance of identity and choice, and once you begin to acknowledge and declare, a number of habits, qualities and practices can trigger the manifestation of God's blessing and cause you to experience higher dimensions of it in your life. These include:

## i. Honoring the Word of God

*Blessed is the man that walketh not in the counsel of the ungodly, nor standeth in the way of sinners, nor sitteth in the seat of the scornful. But his delight is in the law of the LORD; and in his law doth he meditate day and night.*

*And he shall be like a tree planted by the rivers of water, that bringeth forth his fruit in his season; his leaf also shall not wither; and whatsoever he doeth shall prosper.* Psalms 1: 1-3 KJV

Doing and meditating on the word is the number one trigger of the blessing. Neglecting the Word is tantamount to neglecting the very element that created all things. The Word of God really is the greatest blessing God has given us, for nothing can empower and energize you more for your destiny and purpose than the Word. In Joshua 1: 8 God declared an eternal blessing for those who love and practice His Precepts:

*This book of the law shall not depart out of thy mouth; but thou shalt meditate therein day and night, that thou mayest observe to do according to all that is written therein: for then thou shalt make thy way prosperous, and then thou shalt have good success.*

## ii. Service to authority

*Now therefore take, I pray thee, thy weapons, thy quiver and thy bow, and go out to the field, and take me some venison;*
*And make me savoury meat, such as I love, and bring it to me,* **that I may eat; that my soul may bless thee** *before I die.* **Gen 27:3-4 KJV**

You can access higher degrees of blessedness by serving a man or woman in authority. Some children attract more of their parents' blessing by offering them more services and obedience than their brothers and sisters do. Some people have seen their lives and ministries soar to new heights after they did a service to a man of God who then declared powerful words over them. In case your authorities—parent, spouse, pastor, etc.—are not in the habit of blessing people around them, I dare you to provoke them to bless you through service.

Make no mistake about it: sometimes you need blessing from a man. God will often use one of his servants to declare words over your life that will propel you into the fulfillment of His purpose for you. Although Abraham had received a promise from God, he still needed Melchisedec to bless him and strengthen him for the rest of the journey. There is a word of blessing that will set you on the path to success. Make sure you don't despise and miss it!

### iii. Giving

Acts 20: 35 says it is more blessed to give than to receive. Giving activates a phenomenon that increases the ability of the giver to create and acquire more of what he has given away. Every act of giving bears the seed of multiplication. Givers are supernaturally empowered for increase:

*Give, and it shall be given unto you; good measure, pressed down, and shaken together, and running over, shall men give into your bosom. For with the same measure that ye mete withal it shall be measured to you again. Luke 6:38 KJV*

Giving for the work of the ministry and tithing equally form a major trigger of finance-related blessing. Malachi 3:10-12 expresses this unequivocally:

*Bring ye all the tithes into the storehouse, that there may be meat in mine house, and prove me now herewith, saith the LORD of hosts, if I will not open you the windows of heaven, and pour you out a blessing, that there shall not be room enough to receive it. And I will rebuke the devourer for your sakes, and he shall not destroy the fruits of your ground; neither shall your vine cast her fruit before the time in the field, saith the LORD of hosts. And all nations shall call you blessed: for ye shall be a delightsome land, saith the LORD of hosts.* **Malachi 3: 10-12 KJV**

It must also be said here that tithing is not just about the material things you give but about your life. Tithing is a test of love and commitment. Tithing is one of the main ways that we put God first in our lives.

## iv. Faithfulness

Proverbs 28: 20 says, "A faithful man shall abound in blessings…" And of course the opposite applies. So if you stop being faithful and walk away from your source of blessedness, your experience of it shall diminish. The end of Proverbs 28:20 says, "…but he who hastens to be rich will not go unpunished". (RSV)

Faithfulness also entails doing what you are supposed to do with skill and conscientiousness. Too many Christians go about their work and ministry with laxity and complacency. A man's work will always cause people to think and say good things about him. Therefore, wherever he goes he is blessed and so is the blessing continuously abounding. This reality is expressed poignantly in Proverbs 22: 29:

*Do you see a man skillful in his work? He will stand before kings; he will not stand before obscure men.* (RSV)

Of course, when your skills abound you are more solicited by the society's most prominent people.

And the more you deliver, the more people say good things about you, and your reputation grows as do your recommendations. And before you know it, these verbal blessings are converted into financial and material increase and even high placements in society.

## v. Seeking

Now the Bible says that we are saved by grace through faith, but it also makes us understand that we need to seek grace.

*Let us therefore come boldly unto the throne of grace that we may obtain mercy, and find grace to help in time of need.* Hebrews 4:16

*Grace and peace be multiplied unto you, through the knowledge of God, and of our Lord Jesus Christ.* 2 Peter 1: 2

Grace has to be found, and you find something by seeking it. In addition, grace can increase and multiply in a person's life. The more of God you know or get into, the more grace is multiplied.

Everything that can be multiplied can diminish as well.

Note that grace addresses who we are just as blessing does. In 2 Corinthians 10: 15, the apostle Paul says that he is what he is by the grace of God, meaning that grace is not just free salvation, healing, forgiveness, etc.—it is also a divine enablement coming upon the life of a man for him to do and become that which God had purposed for him to do and become. And this divine enablement increases wonderfully in the lives of those who wholeheartedly go after it.

Desire this multiplication of grace so your life can become big enough to be a blessing to the nations.

## KEY POINTS

- As children of God, we must understand that we ARE blessed—not future tense, but right now. In Christ, the blessing of Abraham became ours.

- We are ultimately blessed by virtue of who we are in Him, not by virtue of what we have done for Him.

- Life and blessing will not be imposed on you. You will enjoy it only if you deliberately go for it.

- You cannot claim an inheritance you have not even heard of.

- Doing and meditating on the word is the number one trigger of the blessing.

- Neglecting the Word is tantamount to neglecting the very element that created all things.

- God will often use one of his servants to declare words over your life that will propel you into the fulfillment of His purpose for you.

- Every act of giving bears the seed of multiplication. Givers are supernaturally empowered for increase.

- Tithing is not just about the material things you give but about your life. Tithing is a test of love and commitment.

# CHAPTER FOUR

## ESTABLISHING THE CULTURE OF BLESSING

*And the scripture, foreseeing that God would justify the heathen through faith, preached before the gospel unto Abraham, saying, In thee shall all nations be blessed. So then they which be of faith are blessed with faithful Abraham.* **Galatians 3: 7-9 KJV**

If you are born of God and are going to walk with Him, then saying good things must be a part of your life. Anything other than that would be incongruent with who you are and where you came from. Blessing has to be your nature and culture.

If a man who does not know God calls upon God, he is calling for goodness to locate Him. If a man who is sick calls upon God, he is calling for goodness to locate Him. It does not matter where the person is coming from, whether they are from your religion or someone else's, whether they believe in God or not. What they are calling for is blessedness.

And God's will is for us to be the primary channels of His blessing to the world. We must grow in His blessing, and then impact the world with it. Remember, it is His blessing that enables us to become who we are supposed to be and to achieve what we are supposed to achieve. His blessing secures our identity and guarantees our purpose.

Having learnt how to activate and experience it for our own lives in the previous chapter, it is critical that we also learn how to communicate it to others –

family, community and nation – until it becomes our culture. And remember, anyone can bless: parents can bless their children, spouses can bless each other, children can bless their parents, spiritual leaders can bless the people, and on and on. God's culture is to bless. Let's start propagating it.

## The obligation of blessing

We are called to be dispensers of good things. We are bound by our nature to give out the good that is in us. The Bible says:

*He that believeth on me, as the scripture hath said, out of his belly shall flow rivers of living water.* **John 7: 38 KJV**

*A good man out of the good treasure of the **heart** bringeth forth good things: and an evil man out of the evil treasure bringeth forth evil things.* **Matt 12: 35 KJV**

Failing to bless is inconsistent with our nature. The water we receive from the Lord is supposed to flow out as rivers that will water the lives of other people. We must know that being a blessing is mandatory for a believer. That's the reason the Holy

Blessing: The Culture of God

Spirit lives in us.

Blessing was originally made for multiplication and transmission so that as one person blesses, the other person turns to bless another and so on and so forth. It is a cycle. Blessing is how you empower others to be like you and have what you have. Blessing is a means of duplication and increase. Like Moses and Aaron in Numbers 10, failing to bless your children might result in them lighting a strange fire. No matter how anointed you are, your anointing and grace will not be automatically transferred to your kids until you take charge and begin to speak it deliberately over their lives. That's the reason many believers have wayward children, and they keep complaining and even cursing them, instead of aggressively securing their destinies by speaking empowering words over them.

## The medium of blessing: declaration, not supplication

As mentioned in Chapter one, blessing is released through the spoken word; you don't release the blessing by wishing but by saying. Life and death are in the power of the tongue; therefore, you must say something.

Even more surprisingly, blessing is not actually about a prayer you pray—blessings are declarations made, good things said. Neither is it about casting out devils, the two things being totally unrelated. Blessing is when you *say or declare*—not pray or ask for—good things. It is an order you set in place or motion. It is not something you are asking for, but something that you are establishing. Blessing is established. So when I say to my son, "I bless you", I am establishing things in his life. It is different from when I am crying out, "Father, help my child to be upright." That is prayer and, in this case, supplication. But blessing is establishing a good thing:

"This day I declare you top amongst your equals. I declare you intelligent, I declare you beautiful, I declare you the star of your age, I declare you a hero, heaven shall forever rejoice over you, the earth will celebrate you, your barns shall never run dry, whatever your hand touches shall prosper..." All of these are blessings.

## The validation of blessing: sincerity and faith

Blessing is not just saying empty words, but words full of meaning, faith and power. Consider the following passages of Scripture:

*O generation of vipers, how can ye, being evil, speak good things? for* **out of the abundance of the heart** *the mouth speaketh. A good man out of the good treasure of the* **heart** *bringeth forth good things: and an evil man out of the evil treasure bringeth forth evil things.* **Matthew 12: 34-35 KJV**

*For* **with the heart** *man believeth unto righteousness; and with the mouth confession is made unto salvation.* **Romans 10: 10 KJV**

*It is the spirit that quickeneth; the flesh profiteth nothing: the words that I speak unto you,* **they are spirit, and they are life.** **John 6: 63 KJV**

*Who being the brightness of his glory, and the express image of his person, and upholding all things by **the word of his power**, when he had by himself purged our sins, sat down on the right hand of the Majesty on high.* **Hebrews 1:3 KJV**

Friend, you must speak from the heart. And for your words of blessing to become more powerful, you need to fill the treasure of your heart with good things. Leading a dissolute and inconsistent lifestyle will not totally annihilate your ability to bless, but will severely impair it.

God speaks from the foundation of his power and integrity. Similarly, the more you develop personal power, faith and integrity, the more your words of blessing will affect the lives of those over whom you declare them. The words spoken are validated by the integrity and the faith from which they emanate. Your kids won't take your words of blessing seriously if they feel you really are not serious about life yourself, or if they have the impression that what you are declaring is not from your heart of hearts. As a pastor, your words of blessing over members of your congregation will not have much impact if you do not truly believe in your own declaration and build virtue to support it.

What am I saying? You do not have to be a spiritual giant to be able to bless meaningfully and powerfully. All you need is a sincere heart and a firm belief in what you declare, even if you have not experienced it yourself. Belief validates the blessing. The following verse of Scripture nails it on the head:

*We having the same spirit of faith, according as it is written, I believed, and therefore have I spoken; we also believe, and therefore speak.* 2 Corinthians 4: 13 KJV

If you speak in belief, something WILL happen!

### PRACTICING THE BLESSING

Now, let's get to the practical aspects of developing this culture of blessing. There are people in life that you need to bless and receive blessings from. You need to give and receive blessings to and from your spouse. You need to bless your children and your parents. You are required to bless those under your leadership. Making positive declarations must be a part of your life.

## Blessing your spouse

Blessing your spouse is essential to marital happiness and longevity. Really, you cannot hate someone you keep blessing with benevolent words all the time. Words spoken are always the wind that fans the fire of strife and separation. Even if your spouse does not understand this, make sure you reverse the trend by starting to bless. Declare both spiritual and material blessings over them: love for God, spiritual vitality, fertility, business success, promotion at job site, understanding, a forgiving heart, and so on. Wives, instead of nagging and complaining, bless your husbands' pockets and minds so they can lavish you with love and good things. Husbands, declare wisdom, favor, understanding, and all kinds of goodies to your wives! Do this consistently and deliberately.

In one instance, we see how God comes back to bless Sarai. It is strange to realize that Abraham never thought of blessing his wife. It took a blessing from God to activate fertility in her before she could bear Isaac.

*And God said to Abraham, As for Sarai your wife, you shall not call her name Sarai, but her name shall be Sarah.*

*And I will bless her, and give you a son also of her. Yes, I will bless her, and she shall be a mother of nations, kings of people shall be from her.* Genesis 17: 15-16

Abraham did not take the time to bless his wife, so God did it. Had Terah blessed Abraham, the latter would have known he was supposed to bless his wife as well. A husband is to bless his wife, just like a father must bless his children.

## Blessing your children

A lot of people do not bless their children nowadays, leaving their future in the hands of good fortune and bankrupt educational systems. Meanwhile, parents are supposed to participate aggressively in shaping their children's destiny—and blessing them is the way to go.

Whatever you can see in the spirit, you can delegate the power to your children to fulfill it. Blessing empowers the next generation to do more than their predecessors. The best thing you can leave for your children is the blessing. It will shape their destiny and protect their God-given purpose.

The strength of Jesus was the blessing of His Father. The purpose of the blessing is to secure one's identity and destiny.

To illustrate this further, permit me share my story with you. On the day that I was born, my father came into the maternity and was told he had just had a son. Thereupon he exclaimed, "This one shall be a priest and his name shall be *Christian*." He did not go any further than that because he did not know better, but he was wise enough to declare that on the very first day of my life on earth and heaven has honored that declaration till this day. Can you imagine what it would have been like, if the man knew what I know now, and declared "I see Elijah," for example?

A man named Enoch Adeboye is pastoring the largest church on the surface of the earth. He said something that blew my mind. Upon being asked what his secret was, he replied, "Two things: my communion with God and my mother's prayer."

As a little boy, whenever he did a service to his mother, she would call him and say, "Enoch, you have been good to me. The day you will call for one person, two hundred persons will answer you." Today he calls for one person and millions of people answer. He preaches to a two-million-seater church and has seen the largest crowds ever recorded in history, with an unprecedented seven million in attendance in a single convention. And the ministry is currently planning to increase its hosting capacity to ten million. That's how powerful a parent's blessing can be! You may see pastor Adeboye now and think it is just grace that is operating in his life. Of course it is grace, but this grace was activated a long time ago through the blessings of a mother.

So wait no longer! Beginning today, declare to

your children the good you want to see in their lives. You have been too quiet about their lives. It's high time you started using the authority God has given you as a parent to start shaping the lives of your children through words of blessing.

## STAGES OF BLESSING

### i. At the seed level

Everything starts as a seed. God told Abraham his seed would be mighty on the earth. He was blessing Abraham's reins and telling him his decendants would be a special people. He told Jeremiah, "Before I formed thee in the belly I knew thee". This was referring to a stage that precedes the foetal life. All children first start out as seeds in the loins of their parents long before conception. The word *sperm* actually means seed. And if God already knows us at this stage, then that's where blessing should start.

The devil knows that and that is why he is attacking the seed. More and more men today suffer from low sperm count. Even women's seed is targeted. Remember the Bible in Genesis 3 talks about the "seed of the woman". There are things like fibroids and cysts that attack the woman's ovum to hamper fertilization. So whether you are a man or a woman, you should start blessing your seed while you are single. Then as a parent, you should bless your children's seed and teach them to bless their own seed habitually. Reach out to your teenage children and declare to them, "Your seed shall be mighty on the earth". That's a safe way to secure a heritage for your posterity.

### ii. In the womb

Cultures are inculcated and handed down at a very tender age. Like a seed, they grow with the original ingredients of the soil. The earlier we plant the seed, the earlier it develops and the harder it will be to uproot it.

*Before I formed thee in the belly I knew thee; and before thou camest forth out of the womb I sanctified thee, and I ordained thee a prophet unto the nations.* **Jeremiah 1: 5**

Before a child is born, God's purpose is already

clearly defined for him or her. So parents must be sensitive and begin to speak things they feel are related to the embryo's raison d'être. While the father plays a vital role, at this level, it is the woman who has more responsibility for the blessing of the child. This is because she eats with the child, sleeps with the child, walks about with the child, and in fact shares her life with the child. She must be most careful here because at this time whatever she does, feels, senses and says either blesses or curses the child. She must do all she can to be a happy person, so the baby feels loved and welcome.

*Finally, brethren, whatever is true, whatever is honorable, whatever is just, whatever is pure, whatever is lovely, whatever is gracious, if there is any excellence, if there is anything worthy of praise, think about these things.* Philippians 4: 8 RSV

The woman is constrained to think like this. She is not doing this as a favor for anybody but does it because she is responsible for an unborn child. She does this as an obligation as a person who must bless.

But again, the man as well must be an ever present help during the process by speaking to the child, having fellowship with the baby and being supportive to the wife. The baby needs to hear the father's voice and feel his covering presence. It is security to the child.

### iii. At infancy

Blessing is paramount at infancy stage because it is a major part of the foundation on which the life of a child is going to rest.

Let us take the example of our Lord Jesus Christ. God in His infinite wisdom and knowledge did not leave any stone unturned. Even though Mary and Joseph were present, God kept Simeon alive until he received and blessed Jesus, the promised Messiah. (See Luke chapter 2.) He preserved Anna (even when her husband was dead) to give a motherly blessing to His child Jesus. Eight days after Jesus' birth, they were standing there in case Mary and Joseph missed it.

God did this because He must activate what He Himself had done. Come to think of it, what was the prophetic place of Simeon in the storyline? Was he standing as Elijah or as John? What was the reason for Anna being in the scene? The simple reason is that God's culture is blessing, and he can use anyone and anything to put this in place. That is what we are missing.

Now at infancy the father has to come fully into the life of the child since he was not there in the start-up process. The baby needs to feel secure and hear his father speak good words to him: "you are accepted, you are eagerly awaited, you are the one we were expecting, and we celebrate your arrival." Of paramount importance at this stage is the sense of being accepted and welcome that the parents convey to the child. Let this child know that the world has received him as a champion, and that nothing will be able to circumvent his destiny and identity on the earth.

### iv. At adolescence

Adolescence marks an important transition in the life of any human. At this level, we say goodbye to our childhood as we get ready to move into adulthood. In the Jewish tradition, twelve-year-olds go through a ritual referred to as *Bar Mitzvah*, which means "son of the Law", and implies that by this age, the candidate is supposed to be well educated in the matters pertaining to God's Law and purposes. That is why at the age of twelve, Jesus was given permission to discuss with the Teachers of his day without it being considered an extraordinary occurrence. The only thing that was unusual about it was that the twelve-year-old Messiah displayed understanding that challenged even the doctors and was not possibly within the reach of the other boys of that age group.

Now, the *Bar Mitzvah* was a deliberate act of blessing—nothing casual. It was a time when fathers would invite their friends and release the young boys into manhood before all of Israel. For us, applying a similar culture would mean taking the time to declare specific blessings that will secure the life of our kids as they transition to adulthood.

This is the time when you need to reiterate the confidence you have in the teenager. These are times and hours when kids think they are wiser than their parents. All teenagers think that their parents are backward, no matter how wise they really are. The parents are not moving as fast as they, the kids, are. Young people at this stage want to live a life of adventure.

At any rate, teenagers want to feel trusted at this time about their decisions and choices. They are now surrounded by peers and are going to experience enormous pressure from them: the need to belong, dress like everyone else, do what everyone else does and go where everyone else goes. This can be a challenging season for the Christian family, as parents typically don't want their children to move out until they are sure who their friends are.

Since most parents are in a situation where they have not established a culture of blessing, they are left with only one thing: fear. But fear is not a friend, only an afflicting feeling. Worst still, fear will be of no use in your attempt to reach out to your child. If you are not careful, it will cause you to make your kid's life miserable by imposing extremely strenuous and stringent laws on them. Fear will cause you to focus more on monitoring them instead of showing them the trust and acceptance they need, and you might lose their affection in the process.

Meanwhile, your kids' adolescence is, in fact, the time for you to quit being afraid, put on your faith and take charge by blessing them like never before. Make declarations such as these: "as you grow, you shall be unshakable like the baobabs of Africa. You shall be strong, you shall not be removed, and you shall fulfill your destiny." Bless them with stability, steadfastness, faithfulness to God, purity and confidence. Your blessing is your child's greatest defense again the ills that plague the youth of their day.

### v. Before and after wedding

On the eve of their marriage, our son or daughter is supposed to be released with a blessing like that of Rebekah when she was released from the house of Laban. She was released to become a mother: "As Rebekah was in her time, so will you to be on the earth. As Deborah was in her era, so shall you be influential." Whatever be the blessing that comes to your mind as a parent, this is the time you are going to speak it over your daughter because she is about to leave:

*Therefore a man shall leave his father and mother, and shall cleave to his wife: and the two shall become one.* Matthew 19: 5

The above principle equally applies to the woman. This is your daughter moving into her husband's house, and you are sending her forth to represent future generations and be the mother of future generations and someone's wife. So blessings have to be said. The same goes for the departing son.

Unfortunately, since this has not been the culture taught, some parents do it to their children because they think they have been very good and impressive. But it is done because you want to give your son a proper identity. Now on the wedding day, it is left for the priesthood to give the spiritual nuptial blessing on the couple to seal the blessedness and bring heaven into that relationship.

*...a threefold cord is not easily broken.* Ecclesiastes 4: 12b

**vi. When children bless their parents**

The last lap of the blessings comes when the parents are getting old. At this stage, they need to be blessed. Of course, they will be there to bless their grandchildren but they need to be blessed as well. That is the cycle of life.

This important lap is now where the children turn around to be a blessing to their parents. That is why God says in Ephesians 6: 2, "Honor your father and mother. This is the first commandment with a promise". Children blessing their parents is all about honoring them by rendering service to them in recognition of what they have done. As with Moses, it involves holding up their feeble hands so the blessing may continue to flow.

When you bless your parents in this way, they feel confident about the future because are sure it is secured.

*They shall bring forth fruit in old age; they shall be fat and flourishing.* Psalms 92: 14

This is the reality our older persons have to live in. Yet many children miss it. They fail to honor their aging parents who, out of bitterness, begin to reclaim all they have done for their children. Some parents, because they do not know how powerful their words are, say terrible things over their children and this has some consequences in many lives. You see children who eventually never amount to anything because they know deep on the inside of them that their parents cursed them before they died.

A Bible example is when Jacob in Genesis 49 said Reuben was not going to amount to anything, because Reuben had exposed his nakedness. He said:

*Reuben, thou art my first, my might... unstable as water, thou shalt not excel...* Genesis 49: 3-4 KJV

That was it. But then when you follow the story, by the time you get to Deuteronomy 10, Moses will reverse that declaration using the office of the priesthood. That is what we mean by a higher degree in blessings. By his priestly blessing, he declared that Reuben would increase and not fear. He restored Reuben to where he was supposed to be.

That is why it is dangerous not to have a church,

specifically a local church. Some people have argued that it is okay to be part of the universal church. Well, that is okay, but it is not enough. You will miss something because when the spirit is speaking, He is not speaking to the *Church*; He is speaking to the *churches* (see Revelation 1 to 3).

In the local church are fathers, mothers, brothers and sisters, according to Mark 10:29 - 30 which says:

*Jesus said, Truly I say to you, There is no man who has given up house, or brothers, or sisters, or mother, or father, or children, or land, because of me and the good news, Who will not get a hundred times as much now in this time, houses, and brothers, and sisters, and mothers, and children, and land—though with great troubles; and, in the world to come, eternal life.*

When your biological family has rejected and cursed you, in the church you will have fathers and mothers who can reverse that curse and reposition you in God's blessed purpose for your life.

### The Table of Blessings

The communion table is a table of blessing. The

commemoration of the price paid for our sin is a blessing. We are not celebrating death, we are celebrating our salvation, mightily wrought by the sacrifice of our Lord Jesus.

Communion is not just commemoration. The Lord Jesus Himself instituted it for New Testament believers to access the full benefits of His sacrifice. The Holy Communion causes the full force of His perfect Work on the Cross to become a reality in our lives. Because His body was broken, ours will be preserved. Because His blood was shed, our lives are untouchable.

The Holy Communion should, therefore, be a regular practice among Christians—not a sporadic event in Church. The Jews would do it every Friday, before Sabbath, and we should do it at least as often as that. It is a table of blessings for the entire family and the community that partakes in it.

Sadly, many of us Christians today rather use the Holy Communion to condemn people. Somebody is born again and they will not partake in the communion until they are baptized or are one year old in the faith! Where did we get such doctrines? I think this is one of the most absurd doctrinal fabrications, because the Holy Communion is the celebration of our salvation and should be our privilege from the moment we believe. As a matter of fact, you should be celebrating your salvation every day. Holy Communion used to be a family feast which reminds Jews of deliverance from captivity and to us deliverance from the legal captivity of Satan and hell. There was no condition apart from being a member of the family. The Jews did it in Egypt on the night they were delivered from the hands of their oppressors. After that night, no Jew went into captivity again. So they were celebrating the liberation from captivity. God asked them to get ready while they were taking communion, to wear their best clothes and tie their belts being ready to move out. They were free, never to be bound again.

I exhort you therefore to make the Holy Communion a regular practice in your home with your entire family. Doing this sporadically has robbed many generations of Christians of the riches of God's blessings. It is high time we reversed this trend.

*       *       *

**I declare the following blessings over your life:**

You are blessed by God and can never be cursed. You are a blessing to others and because of you many shall find joy and fulfillment.

By the covenant of life you have in Jesus and by the testament of your Father God, you are blessed in the blessing line of Abraham, wherein he that blesses you is blessed and he that curses you is cursed.

Because Jesus was made a curse so that you may be a blessing, you are blessed indeed with the goodness of God. You are the manifestation of the blessing of God to the world and an example of the beauty of God.

You shall always be top over your equals and in your coming in and going out, you shall see the fruit of your labor. By reason of this reality, your blessing is higher than any covenant. You are blessed in the morning, blessed in the afternoon, blessed in the evening and blessed all round. You are blessed in your family and marriage. You are blessed in your job. You are blessed in your career. You are blessed in your education. You are blessed in your investments and businesses. You are blessed in your ministry. You are a distributor of blessings. You are the head and not the tail, a conqueror and an overcomer. You are blessed forever. In Jesus' name!

## KEY POINTS

- God's will is for us to be the primary channels of His blessing to the world.
- Failing to bless is inconsistent with our nature. The water we receive from the Lord is supposed to flow out as rivers that will water the lives of other people.
- No matter how anointed you are, your anointing and grace will not be automatically transferred to your kids until you take charge and begin to speak it deliberately over their lives.
- Blessing is not just saying empty words, but words full of meaning, faith and power.
- Blessing your spouse is essential to marital happiness and longevity. You cannot hate someone you keep on blessing.
- Your blessing is your child's greatest defense against the ills that plague the youth of their day.

- Blessing empowers the next generation to do more than their predecessors. The best thing you can leave for your children is the blessing.
- Children blessing their parents is all about honoring them by rendering service to them in recognition of what they have done.
- The Holy Communion should be a regular practice among Christians—not a sporadic event in Church.
- When your biological family has rejected and cursed you, in the church you will have fathers and mothers who can reverse that curse and reposition you in God's blessed purpose for your life.

# CHAPTER FIVE

## Hindrances to the Blessing

*I have set before you life and death, blessing and cursing. Therefore, choose life, so that both you and your seed may live. Deuteronomy 30: 19.*

Once more, we can see from the above Scripture that blessing ultimately is a choice. While we are advised to go for it, some people, unfortunately, choose the other road, embracing a lifestyle that circumvents the manifestation of God's and man's blessing in their lives. Discussed below are three major issues you must watch out against in order to keep the blessing activated in your life.

## 1. Ignoring the Word of God

*My people are destroyed for lack of knowledge. Because you have rejected knowledge, I also will reject you from being priest for Me; Because you have forgotten the law of your God, I also will forget your children.* Hosea 4:6-7.

Ignoring the word of God hinders our blessings. One of the tragedies of the Church in this age is our rejection of God's Word. Do you still spay attention to what God says and wants? Too many Believers have embraced ignorance and ludicrous doctrines instead of the undiluted, omnipotent Word of our God. As a result, the glory that the Church is supposed to walk in has remained veiled. We see in the above passage of Hosea that even though the people had glory, the Lord turned it into shame because of their refusal of His ways. Our blessing is in His Word. Church, go back to the Word!

## 2. Denial of identity

Denial of identity corrupts the blessing. The Bible is filled with instances of blessings conferred mostly on the basis of identity. Adam, Noah and Abraham are good examples of this. But we will focus on Jacob's blessing.

The account in Genesis 32 tells the story of a man who lived a life that was not his and bore the name and blessing of someone else. His father blessed him as Esau and not Jacob. By this, he assumed the trouble that was meant for Esau because he had usurped the identity of the latter. This meant that anything that was attached to Esau became his.

Now, this further illustrates the fact that we are blessed for identity and not for our works, as Jacob was blessed not just because of the meal he prepared—even though this was a trigger— but because he was IDENTIFIED as Esau. Genesis 27: 19:

*And Jacob said to his father, I am Esau your first-born...*

However, years later, when Jacob left Laban's

house, he had an encounter with an angelic presence. In this theophanic occurence, something changed significantly in his life. He wrestled with the angel and at dawn, as the angel was getting ready to go, Jacob insisted that he must bless him.

*And He said, Let Me go, for the day breaks. And he said, I will not let you go except You bless me.*

An interesting point here is the question of the angel:

*And He said to him, what is your name? And he said, Jacob.* Gen 32: 26-27

Finally, in this encounter, Jacob comes to grips with who he really was. Because he had not been living with the right identity, he had not been experiencing his God-ordained blessedness. The moment he reaffirmed his identity, he started flowing in the blessing. Child of God, hold on to your indentity in Christ Jesus, not on what your country or tribe says you are! Your new identity is in Christ, so you can no longer be defined by your earthly or social origins. The mistake of Jacob was to think that he would enjoy life better in someone else's shoes, whereas his blessing was tied to his God-given identity. Make sure you hold fast to God's definition of you!

## 3. Dishonoring father and mother

*Honor your father and your mother, that your days may be long upon the land which the LORD your God is giving you.* Exodus 20: 12

God makes it expressly clear that our fathers and mothers have to be honored and respected. God, being a Father Himself, knows the responsibility and great strength it takes to look after and groom children. As such he asks us to honor these people who not only brought us to the earth, but also raised us and were the channels through which He, God, blessed us.

*Children, obey your parents in the Lord, for this is right. "Honour your father and mother," which is the first commandment with promise: "that it may be well with you and you may live long on the earth."* Ephesians 6: 1-3

We see here that this is the only commandment in the Bible that is accompanied by the blessing of long life. Can you imagine what the opposite of this implies? That dishonoring your father and mother is circumventing the blessings of long life and fulfillment on the earth. No wonder we see instances in the Bible where people had their destinies short-circuited by disobeying this law.

*And it happened, when Israel dwelt in that land, that Reuben went and lay with Bilhah his father's concubine; and Israel heard about it.*

*Now the sons of Jacob were twelve: "Reuben, you are my firstborn, My might and the beginning of my strength, The excellency of dignity and the excellency of power. Unstable as water, you shall not excel, Because you went up to your father's bed; Then you defiled it -He went up to my couch.* Genesis 35: 22 and 49: 3-4.

When Jacob's time to depart had come and he gathered his sons to bless them, he did something unusual to Reuben. He started to describe the blessing of Reuben. He said Reuben was his might and strength. He was the excellency of dignity and the excellency of his power. What tremendous blessings! He was blessed with leadership and power, an epitome of royalty and glory.

However, the next passage is rather disheartening and unfortunate. Jacob said because Reuben had slept with his father's concubine on his bed, thereby defiling it, he was going to be unstable as water and would never excel. What a demotion! What a sad fate for a man destined for greatness and royalty!

How many people in our world today have attracted such misfortunes because of disobeying and dishonoring their parents? Make sure you never fall into this trap!

*I call Heaven and earth to record today against you. I have set before you life and death, blessing and cursing. Therefore, choose life, so that both you and your seed may live.* Deuteronomy 30: 19

Being blessed is about choosing to be blessed. **You must make up your mind that you are going to walk in God's blessing.**

# FINAL WORDS

## THE CHURCH OF THE FATHER

The Lord Jesus introduced the world into a new era where mankind can have access to God as a Father. Jesus himself never called God God, except on the Cross. The rest of the time, He called God Father, and this unique relationship conferred upon Him an identity that set Him apart from all prophets before Him. This higher identity meant higher authority and blessing. Consequently, the Church should experience higher authority and blessing by virtue of this Father-sons relationship that we have be introduced to through our Lord Jesus Christ. Think about it: the One Israel calls God is not just your God but your very own Father.

The last-day Church of Jesus Christ will be the *Church of the Father*, just as the last son of Jacob was the son of the Father. The Church of the Father is the Church of the Right Hand, for the Son is seated at His right hand of power, and as such, we enjoy a much higher level of blessedness than any other group of people in the world.

Let us therefore quit any form of godliness that denies the power of God, according to 2Timothy 3: 5. Our Christianity must set us on top of the world. That is our heritage and calling.

We need to appropriate this truth and run with it vigorously, especially in this end time when the kingdom of darkness is beginning to gain grounds. This radical call for action is not negotiable, nor is it to be compromised because our mind and soul—where the Kingdom of God resides—are constantly under attack by forces of hell that want to besiege and possess it. Hence the biblical warning:

*And from the days of John the Baptist until now the kingdom of heaven suffereth violence, and the violent take it by force.* **Matthew 11: 12 KJV.**

We must therefore appropriate and make use of the grace of God that has been lavished abundantly on us in this dispensation, and remain steadfast in the faith by which salvation is made available.

*For the grace of God that brings salvation has appeared to all men.* **Titus 2: 11**

We are in that dispensation where God is raising a new breed of people and most specifically a people that are zealous unto good works. We are in those days prophesied by Isaiah in chapters 37: 32 and 9: 7 where he said the zeal of the Lord would perform this.

We must enter into the new order where benediction is the norm and blessing is the culture. Where our words are seasoned with salt and our declarations are coated with God's mind for every situation. We must run with this truth we have received and experience the realities of this sweet godly system so that our fruits and our breed may be distinguished on the earth. We must run with this culture and correct the punitive culture that many countries, mostly in Africa and in Cameroon in particular, have run with and that has put the people under low self-esteem, limited mind-set, poverty mentality, and curses.

So in spite of whatever doctrine you may have followed over the years, I charge you always to remember and broadcast one indisputable truth, one phrase, one belief, one practice and one system:

**BLESSING IS GOD'S CULTURE, AND IT SHOULD BE YOURS TOO.**

## About the Author

**Rt. Rev. Dr. Christian Raymond Ngwu** is one of the most gifted and celebrated Church fathers in the nation of Cameroon with an undeniable international influence. He is a certified life coach and mentor to many mentors. With close to three decades of leadership and ministerial experience, he has remained one of the most trusted Spiritual fathers to thousands of young and upcoming leaders and pastors in the nation of Cameroon and beyond. He is the president of the *International Pastoral Assembly of Africa (IPAA)* and the presiding Bishop of *Living Word Fellowship International*. He is married to Reverend Mrs Laurentine Ngwu and they are blessed with children.

Blessing: The Culture of God

www.ingramcontent.com/pod-product-compliance
Lightning Source LLC
Chambersburg PA
CBHW060950040426
42445CB00011B/1094